New Zealand
Gift of the Sea

NEW ZEALAND

GIFT OF THE SEA

Brian Brake : PHOTOGRAPHS

Maurice Shadbolt : TEXT

WHITCOMBE AND TOMBS, PUBLISHERS : NEW ZEALAND, AUSTRALIA, LONDON

NOTE: Commentaries on the Photographs will be found beginning on page 142 and Acknowledgments on the flap following page 147. The List of Photographs is on the inside of this same flap, which may be left open for ready reference while looking through the book.

ISBN 0 7233 0228 6

Published by Whitcombe and Tombs, a division of Whitcoulls Ltd., Christchurch / Printed in Japan for John Weatherhill, Inc., production and design consultants / Copyright © 1963 by Brian Brake and Maurice Shadbolt / First edition, October 1963 / Third impression (revised), May 1964 / Sixth impression (revised), December 1973

When we first prepared this book in 1963 we wanted a volume with few facts and fewer figures. With word and picture we tried to show the New Zealand that was and the New Zealand that is—in hope that some might glimpse, within these pages, the New Zealand that yet may be. We hardly expected so huge a response to our project for so long, and could never have imagined that ten years later our work would still be needed to show New Zealand to New Zealanders, and our country to the world. This revised version, then, has tried to catch up with a decade in which New Zealand has fast grown as a distinctive Pacific nation. We hoped, once, to help that growth; our satisfaction now is that we survive to confirm it. We first dedicated this book to those New Zealanders, the length of the country, who made our work possible. That dedication still stands.

BRIAN BRAKE
MAURICE SHADBOLT

In the beginning a green land lay empty. Far to the north a rocky finger of land beckoned vainly into the vast Pacific. Washed by great seas, this shore knew only the language of seabirds. Elsewhere, civilizations had risen and fallen, Christ had come and gone from the earth, but here the land still waited for the first human voice. . . .

Wild winds and wilder water carried the voyaging Polynesians

to these lonely beaches. . . .

. . . They first saw land as a long white cloud.

Yet it was still a land

of great silences for the first Europeans. . . .

. . . *For the pioneers*
there was wilderness
to be won.

In hostile highlands they built homesteads . . .

. . . and everywhere
      they built churches.

Fired or felled, the forest gave way to crop and pasture . . .

. . . and

the land began to tame

  its restless tamer.

Simply by sailing in a new direction
You could enlarge the world.
—ALLEN CURNOW

NEW ZEALAND BEGINS with sea and ends with sea. Understand this and you begin to comprehend New Zealand and the New Zealander. The thundering surf is our frontier. And our only frontier guards, gulls and migratory birds. With justice, then, the Polynesian voyagers called the land *Tiritiri o te Moana*—the gift of the sea.

When the first man walked erect upon the earth, New Zealand was already a treasure locked in a vast ocean. A million years or more would pass before human eyes glimpsed its rocky headlands, long beaches, high mountains.

Who those earliest people were we do not know. Some Maori legends tell of an explorer called Kupe who returned to his home in the Society Islands to tell of a great land to the south. Even the first European is in doubt. He may have been a Frenchman, or the Spaniard Juan Hernandez. But beyond all doubt, towards noon on December 13, 1642, the Dutch explorer Abel Tasman sighted "a large land, uplifted high". He was off the west coast of the South Island, and what he actually saw was the great white rampart of the Southern Alps rising above dense green rain forest.

For Tasman it seemed the fulfilment of a dream. He imagined he was looking at the fabled "Beach" of which Marco Polo first heard in China, the great southern continent which Sir Francis Drake and others had sought in vain. The sad truth was that, to find a continent, Tasman had arrived millions of years too late. The islands of New Zealand, not truly oceanic, are what is left of a great continent geologists call Gondwanaland. It vanished in a time unimaginably remote.

These islands;
the remnant peaks of a lost continent,
roof of an old world, molten droppings
from earth's bowels, gone cold;
ribbed with rock, resisting the sea's corrosion
for an age, and an age to come.
—A. R. D. FAIRBURN

NEW ZEALAND'S LAST land bridges sank beneath the Pacific before the earliest mammals began to occupy the earth. And evolution, in these lost islands, was to follow a distinctly wayward path.

Three-quarters of New Zealand's original vegetation is not to be found elsewhere in the world. Until the Polynesians brought the rat and the dog, bats and seals were the only mammals.

Strange flightless birds soon occupied the positions held elsewhere by mammals. There was the great moa, hunted to extinction by the Maori and surely one of the most wonderful birds of all time—it grew as high as an African elephant and grazed on grassland; there was the notornis, or takahe, long thought extinct like the moa until the discovery of a colony in an unexplored region of the South Island a few years ago. And above all there was the shy, bush-foraging kiwi, which was, when men welded a nation, to become a symbol of nationhood.

Yet some of the world's most ancient forms of life have also persisted in these islands. New Zealand has the most primitive living frog in the world, a form of tremendous antiquity going back perhaps 170 million years; and the country's only notable reptile, the tuatara lizard, with its vestigial third eye, is also the world's most archaic. It belongs to a time before giant dinosaurs roamed the earth.

> *But the mountain still lives out that fiercer life*
> *Beneath its husk of darkness; blind to the age*
> *Scuttling by it over shiftless waters,*
>
> *The cold beams that wake upon its headlands*
> *To usher night-dazed ships. For it belongs to*
> *A world of fire before the rocks and waters.*
> —CHARLES BRASCH

THE LAND STILL CREAKED and swayed with earthquake, quivering with its newness; hot upthrown rock climbed towards the sky, accepting cool mantles of snow. Volcanoes spouted, and jagged cliffs lifted crazily from the sea.

Then the land grew calm after the tumult of time. A mountain collapsed here, a harbour opened there. But these were only finishing touches. Cold inland lakes took the colour of the sky, and fierce waves, pounding rock to sand, were made phosphorescent by a Pacific moon. Scrub, creeper, and tree flowered about the cooled craters.

Without challenge, the forest grew even more thick and tangled. This was a land still so young that the trees had not yet learnt to shed their leaves. And the flowers were barely famil ar with the artifice of scent.

26

So long protected by the sea from other land, there was no bitter rivalry, little harsh competition, in the natural world of these islands. There was not the necessity to change or perish. All things adapted gently. And in time even the birds, blown here from far lands, became uniquely New Zealand's.

This then was the strange green land which knew no human footprint until after the rise and fall of Greece and Rome, until after the life of Christ.

It was ready for man. But who would receive it, this gift of the sea?

Clearly it was something to be earned only by the boldest of men. For New Zealand is twelve hundred miles from the coast of Australia and six thousand miles from Asia or the Americas. Around it rage some of the world's wildest waters.

Perhaps, more than a thousand years ago, only the Polynesians could have found it. They were already the greatest breed of sea-wanderers the world has ever known. There was scarcely a speck of habitable land in the entire eastern Pacific which they had not claimed as their own.

It has been a fashion to decry the mighty voyage of the Polynesians, to explain away their occupation of the Pacific as a series of accidents. What a magnificent series of accidents then! Europeans on the Atlantic coast were maritime peoples too. Yet islands like Madeira, only 330 miles west of Africa, and the Azores, 800 miles west of Portugal, were not discovered by Europeans until the fifteenth century. But, centuries before, the Polynesians had roamed most of the Pacific— perhaps even reaching South America—after their original journey out of Asia.

Of course the first discovery of New Zealand must have been an accident. Some crew of Polynesians, blown like thistledown across the empty ocean, found a horizon filled with a mysterious coast. It was the last major area of habitable, fertile land left vacant in the world.

New Zealand is sometimes spoken of as the last frontier of the new world. This is a very European idea. It was really something more. It was the last frontier for the human race itself. The last place for man to try again.

Haven of hunger; landfall of hope.
—A.R.D. FAIRBURN

THE REST IS A MATTER for conjecture; it is probable that we will never know the answers. Perhaps those first voyagers returned to their tropical homeland, as the legend of Kupe suggests, to tell of a new land to the south. And perhaps descendants of those people, driven out of their over-crowded islands by tribal warfare, did set out in search of *Tiritiri o te Moana*. They may have manned canoes for the south, generation after generation, only to find slow death from thirst or starvation on the treacherous, unpredictable Pacific.

Certainly some Maori legends are definite. Kupe, these say, found New Zealand in about A.D. 925. Versions of the story disagree about whether the country was inhabited. A descendant of Kupe, named Toi, sailed down to New Zealand about 1150 to find the country already inhabited. But by whom? The legends grow vague. A century or two later a great fleet of canoes is supposed to have sailed from the Society Islands to New Zealand. These voyagers are said to have first seen the land as a long white cloud on the horizon, and they gave it the name of *Aotearoa*—land of the long white cloud.

Present evidence tends to confirm some—but only some—of this story. It indicates that New Zealand was in fact uninhabited before the fourth century A.D. But it also suggests that by the year 1000 there was in existence a settled life already a few centuries old.

Was there really a sudden influx, a great fleet? Some modern scholars think not; they maintain that there never was intentional migration; that it is unlikely New Zealand was settled by the occupants of a great fleet of canoes from the Society Islands.

Yet I remember vividly a conversation I once had on the subject with a proud old Maori:

"We can still trace back our *whakapapa*—our genealogy—to the voyagers of the great fleet," he said, "to the men of the *Tainui, Aotea, Takitumu,* and all the other canoes."

What then, I asked, was I to believe?

"There are some things we shall never know," he answered. "Our truth—of Kupe and the great voyages—is the truth of poetry. Poetry is always the greater truth."

Perhaps he is right, despite archaeology and carbon-dating. These old Maori legends, the history that changed subtly to poetry on the lips of the old storytellers, will be remembered so long as there is a New Zealand.

> *This is my canoe. Let it leap up, let it fly,*
> *Let it fly to the beginning of the earth,*
> *Let it fly to the land discovered by Kupe,*
> *To the land settled by Toi.*
> —TRADITIONAL INCANTATION

INDICATIONS ARE THAT there were probably two groups of arrivals. Of the earliest Polynesians, now called "moa hunters", we know little. They speak to us only through a few amulets and pendants of strange beauty, and through faded paintings, in remote caves, that may be their work. Of the later, more highly developed Polynesians, currently called the "classic" or "Fleet" Maori, we know more. Unlike their gentle predecessors, they were skilled in war. And after they scattered, swamped, or absorbed the earliest occupants of the land, they evolved an impressive culture.

It's still not impossible in New Zealand today to imagine oneself back to the time of the first men. Walking lonely beaches, following tracks high into dense bush country, the New Zealander can still see the land much as the first men saw it.

How did it affect them, change them? For one thing the climate was more rigorous, life more demanding. They must often have remembered wistfully, in times of frost or snow or bitter winter wind, their lost tropical homeland. The beaches were not fringed with coconut palms. It is probable that they did try, unsuccessfully, to introduce the coconut, and they did carry with them, from their islands, the gourd, the taro, the yam, and the kumara or sweet potato.

They also brought the paper mulberry tree, from which tapa cloth is woven for clothing in the tropics. But no matter how they nursed and protected the plant, it did not flourish; it barely survived, and anyway tapa was thin protection against New Zealand winters. So they turned, in their new islands, to the native flax. From this they wove garments, baskets, and rope.

In this way, and in many others, they came to terms with the new land. They adapted. New Zealanders, brown or white, have always been quick to adapt and improvise. Isolation has made it a matter of necessity.

Yet there were compensations. If vegetable food was hard to win from the bush, the trees were clamorous with birds. And the sea was rich in fish.

Physically, then, they may have made themselves quickly at home. Spiritually, it was another matter. They had to absorb a new land, the greatest in Polynesia, into their cosmic scheme of things—a new land with all its mysteries.

And there were mysteries in plenty. Mountains, capped with perpetual snow, the like of which they had never seen. Great dry plains where only tough tussock and spiky matagouri grew. Volcanoes which, in eruption, threatened to split the very land apart. Jets of boiling water hissing up to a thousand feet above the forest. Great frozen rivers cracking, tumbling in the summer heat. Caves, lighted only by glowing insects, winding eerily into the underworld. Bush as thick and tangled as anything the tropics ever knew, and roaring rivers that were wider, swifter. Immense beaches, sweeping eighty miles without a break, where men grew tiny at dusk.

It must all have required a mighty effort to comprehend.

So they named each place, each mystery, and tried to make account. This was necessary, even if only for comfort's sake: a man likes to rest easy, without too much fear, when the red sun dies each evening on a darkening land.

From central Polynesia they had brought a complex system of belief; in New Zealand this theology grew even more elaborate. Old gods assumed new shapes, new relatives; levels of knowledge mounted and in the twelfth sky, above all other gods, dwelt a supreme deity named Io.

Perhaps stimulated by the temperate climate, the Maori created the most advanced and complex culture in all Polynesia. Here an old craft, like wood carving, developed into something more; and with dazzling new raw materials, like South Island greenstone and the totara of the forest, the Maori made rich and often stunning art. Buildings and war canoes were intricately sculptured; the designs are not to be found elsewhere in Polynesia. But perhaps their most beautiful creations were those worked from greenstone, a type of jade to be found only in the South Island. To obtain it they travelled hundreds of miles by canoe and traversed rugged, snow-covered passes. They carried it away to the furthest north, where fragments can still be picked up in bush or sandhills today. The Maori name for the South Island was *Te Wai Pounamu*—the water of jade.

The North Island was *Te Ika a Maui*—the fish of Maui. A folk-hero to be found in many Polynesian legends, Maui won repute by bringing fire to earth and taming the sun; he perished only when he sought to bring immortality to mankind. Certainly, in fishing the North Island up from the ocean to the dismay of his brothers, he created an all-time angling record. His jealous brothers hacked at the fish in their bad temper, and this explains the North Island's rugged aspect.

Maori population was thicker in the warm north; defeated tribes tended to occupy the colder landscape of the south. Yet, if purely regional legends are any indication, most Maoris comprehended the nature of the entire country. I remember as a child being fascinated by the legends of my district, their geographic intricacy; relatively minor local legends might also take into account glaciers six hundred miles to the south. In all New Zealand there is hardly a hill, mountain, river or valley which was not known and named.

Even today, there are few European New Zealanders who can see their country clear and whole as the Maoris did. Our vision is fragmented. For one pakeha, New Zealand may mean the great spaces of the high country, tussock plain and snow mountain; for another, white beaches lined with crimson-flowered pohutukawa, or muddy tidal creeks tangled with mangroves. Yet others may see New Zealand as inland valleys patterned with pasture, silent lakes, limestone canyons decked with toi-toi plumes.

But for the Maori, *Tiritiri o te Moana* or *Aotearoa*—"gift of the sea" or "land of the long white cloud"—was all of a piece.

Of course, with very natural human arrogance, they may have thought, in knowing and naming, that they had taken possession of the land. But in reality the land had taken possession of them.

> *. . . their touch was light; warm in their hearts holding*
> *The land's image, they had no need to impress themselves*
> *Like conquerors, scarring it with vain memorials.*
> *They had no fear of being forgotten.*
> —CHARLES BRASCH

Now NEW VOYAGERS cruised the Pacific. First Tasman and then, some 120 years later, Captain James Cook. Before long, white sails began to multiply along the coast; soon European settlements began to straddle the landscape.

Europeans were slow to make sense of this strange race of cannibals and poets, artists and warriors, orators and myth-makers. And before it was all over the colour of brave blood would stain the soil. In the explosion the old gods perished.

> *Where are they?*
> *I call, but there is no sound.*
> *The tide ebbs*
> *Silently away.*
>
> *Memories rise in the still air*
> *Like smoke from many fires.*
> *Is this the same place,*
> *This place of ashes?*
> —RARAWA KEREHOMA

TOWARDS THE END of the nineteenth century the Maori race, still diminishing in number, was pronounced doomed. A people once a quarter million strong were now a mere 43,000. Today the Maori population is nearly six times that figure, and it is growing at a much faster rate than that of other New Zealanders.

Here is a remarkable people, a race that refused to die.

Voyaging out of Asia into the sunrise, Poly-
nesians made the Pacific their home.
As they multiplied they sought
new land, new islands.
Wind, current, and stars guided them across
the ocean. Then gliding birds and
floating leaves summoned
them to a strange,
haunted shore. . . .

*A land ruled by gods—by tall Tane and
turbulent Tangaroa—a land
of many mysteries.*

*In the
shadow of
the past
the Maori
still grows . . .*

. . . for the past is more than a thing of dreams:

it is still something for pride.

Now there are new adventures beside the marvels of the past.

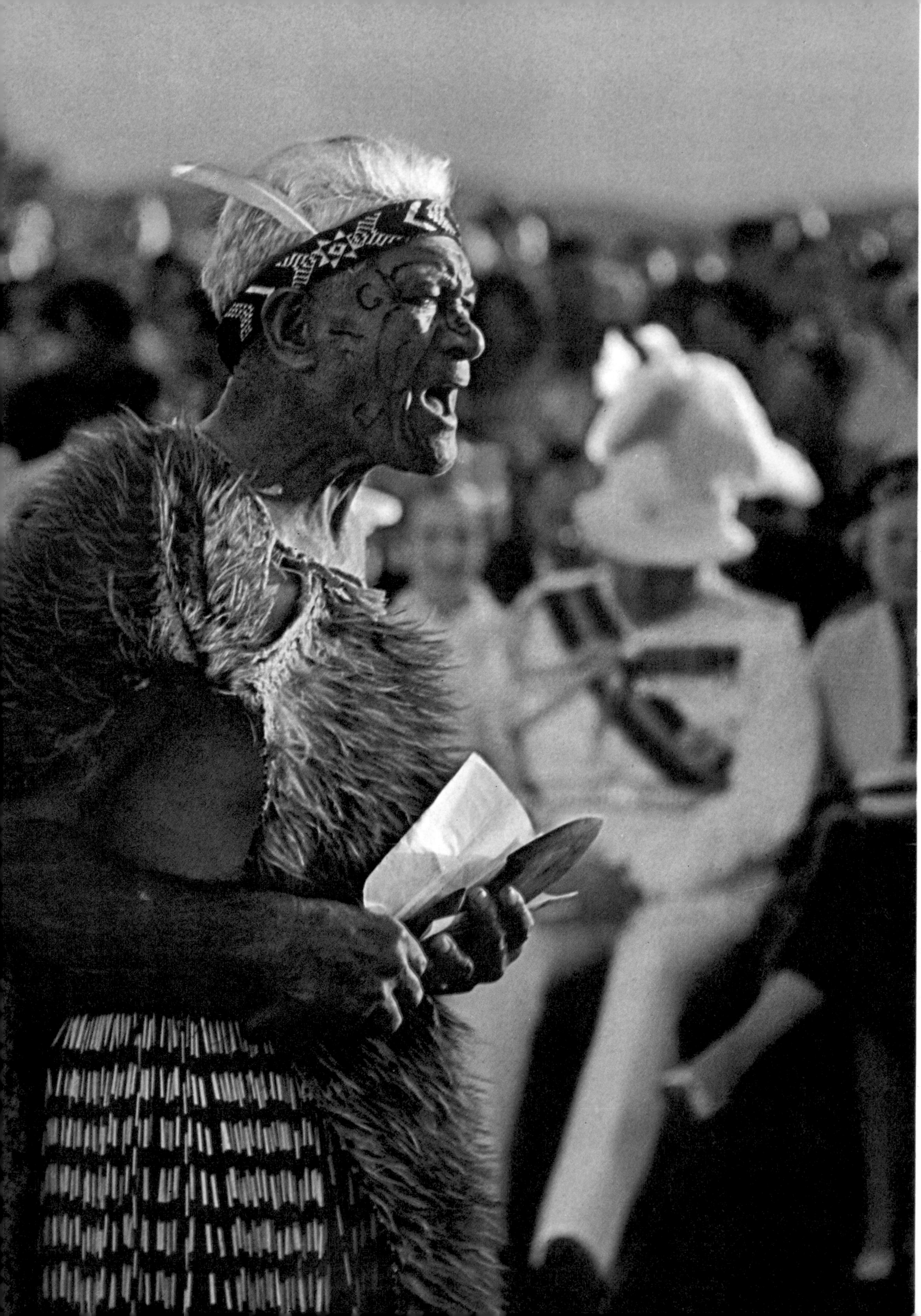

What binds a race is spirit . . .

. . . *and
what gives
strength
is pride.*

56

A portion of the Treaty of Waitangi, signed in 1840 by Lieutenant-Governor William Hobson and Maori chieftains. By this treaty many tribes ceded their sovereignty to Queen Victoria. In return they were guaranteed possession of their lands, forests, and fishing grounds and were given the rights and privileges of British subjects. With its imperfections, the document did not prevent the differences between the races, mainly over land, from developing into bloody warfare, but it has stood as a guiding principle for men of good will on both sides, and in time came to be regarded as the Magna Carta of the Maori race.

No continent appeared;
It was something different, something
Nobody counted on.
                                        —ALLEN CURNOW

NO ONE WAS IN A HURRY to claim New Zealand.

If legend is to be believed, Kupe sailed home after his discovery and his descendants took another two hundred years to come back. Abel Tasman, the first known European, didn't even set foot on the land his countrymen eventually named *Nieuw Zeeland*. It wasn't altogether for want of trying; he lost four men in a clash with Maoris during one attempt to land. After Cook's rediscovery in 1769, the great southern continent shrank to three islands on the world's maps; and no one appeared especially enthusiastic. Comparatively empty, Australia had obvious value as a dumping ground for convicts. But what use was there in islands with a population of fierce Maoris? True, the timber was good, and the country made a base and dubious haven for those whalers and sealers who chanced cannibal attack. In the 1830's the British dillied, the French dallied, and finally in 1840 the Union Jack was hoisted as a half-hearted gesture towards the North Island Maoris. To forestall the French the flag was flown in the South Island too.

And the first immigrant ships were arriving.

Yet nations usually take longer to make up their minds than individuals; and New Zealand was already the home of many bold spirits of European descent. True, some were missionaries in the line of duty; but many of these missionaries went far beyond the call of duty in their efforts to explore and comprehend a new land. There were adventurers who sought freedom, democrats and idealists who wished to build utopia. There were traders out for quick fortunes. And there were refugees from the tyranny of whaling ships, escaped convicts from Australia.

These European firstcomers, and their reasons for coming, offer a clue to New Zealand's character. For the country has meant many things to many men—escape, duty, opportunity, freedom, utopia, or refuge.

It can still mean many of these things today.

. . . the seeds of the race, the forerunners:
offshoots, outcasts, entrepreneurs,
architects of Empire, romantic adventurers;
and the famished, the multitude of the poor. . . .

They shouted at the floating leaf,
laughed with joy at the promise of life,
hope becoming belief, springing
alive, alight, gulls at the masthead crying,
the crag splitting the sky, slowly
towering out of the sea, taking
colour and shape, and the land
swelling beyond; noises
of water among rocks, voices singing.
—A.R.D. FAIRBURN

Now SHIP AFTER SHIP discharged pale human cargo on this barbarian shore. Some sought to grow crops, others to harvest gold. For all it meant a new beginning.

That the country was truly the last frontier of the new world was demonstrated by the American pioneers who pushed the frontier westward to California and, finding they could push it no further, took ship to New Zealand in search of gold; many stayed to farm or trade. Like America or Australia, New Zealand has always offered a refuge and a wealth of space. In a land area comparable with that of Britain or Japan, New Zealand today has only three million people against Britain's sixty million and Japan's hundred million.

There's a myth, fostered by sentimentalists at home and widely accepted abroad, that New Zealand is one hundred percent British, more English than England. The myth conveniently overlooks the Bohemians, the Dalmatians and Danes, the Italians and Greeks and Chinese and Indians who arrived last century. Nor does it take into account the thousands of Dutchmen, Germans, Hungarians, Poles, and other East Europeans who have arrived since the war. All these groups have diversified New Zealand society, particularly in the cities; and even in the countryside the Dalmatians, for example, with their vineyards and orchards, have made parts of the North Island look very much their own.

To say nothing of the more than three hundred thousand Polynesians—mostly native Maoris, but also Samoans, Tongans, Cook and Tokelau islanders. New Zealand has lately begun to take the overflow from many Pacific islands; tropical Polynesians still find the temperate land to the south a place of opportunity. This, and the Maori rate of natural increase, said at times to be the highest of any race in history, means the Polynesian influence is growing ever stronger.

In the 1960s and 1970s the country became haven for Americans and Europeans fleeing racial strife, war fevers and the pollution of earth and air. They found a land short of Utopia in these respects, but still satisfying enough as a place to begin again.

It's true, though, that some of our founding fathers planned a replica of English society here, complete with gentry, rustic labourers, and pantrymaids. A rickety replica it turned out to be. Most of the gentry fled home to England; those who remained often had good reason to stay out of Britain. Of the remittance men and their like, one pioneer newspaper thundered: "These men are not only useless in a colony, they become the pests of society."

So the labourer married the pantrymaid and together they set to work with a will; they didn't have their passage money home anyway. But it wasn't likely that they would want to follow the timid gentry back; here they could start afresh, without castes, without inhibitions.

The mock-English gentility which has patchily survived English colonization, particularly in suburbia, is still too often seen as the real thing by visitors who mistake the frills for the fabric of our society. New Zealand was, and still is, a working man's country. I don't mean that everyone still earns a living by physical sweat. Though it's nothing unusual for a city bank manager, as urban and urbane as they come five days of the week, to strip down to shorts and singlet on a Saturday and work as a carpenter on boat or weekend cottage. After all, the pioneers in his family may be only a generation or two gone.

History tells us they were hard and bold;
They carved out forests and they dug for gold,
But many died young and some died old
And their passionate hearts are quiet and cold
In the early, early days.
—BASIL DOWLING

SWEAT MADE THIS nation—sweat and sometimes blood. For proof I need go no further than my own family history. Of my ancestors, some were idealists, some opportunists; they came out to a raw land last century in whaling boats and crowded immigrant ships. They panned for gold beneath cold southern mountains, and dug kauri gum from the tough clay of the warm north. They hacked farms from the bush, ran sheep, milked cows, and ploughed the blackened soil between burnt-off stumps. They carried rifles in the Maori wars and helped push roads and railways spectacularly around and under mountains. And as they won the wilderness they, and thousands like them, soon became as native as the kiwi.

Wrote the English historian Froude after a visit in 1885: "The English race should not come to New Zealand to renew the town life which they left behind them. They will never grow into a new nation thus. They will grow into a nation when they are settled in their own houses and freeholds, like their forefathers who drew bow in Agincourt and trailed pike in the wars of the Commonwealth; when they own their own acres, raise their own crops, their own sheep and cattle. . . ."

Froude was right, but from the earliest times Europeans had, from necessity, already conformed to his prescription for a nation. Crop-raisers, sheepmen and cattlemen, men with leathery hands and aggressive stance; they are the rock on which a prosperous nation has been built. Without them New Zealand might still be struggling into the twentieth century, still a poor colony of England. Instead, nearly seventy years a nation, New Zealand has become one of the world's more reasonably advanced and just societies. And our wealth, without which we could have achieved little, continues to come from the land.

Today, within easy reach of New Zealand's growing cities, the spiritual descendants of the pioneers can still be found. They may call themselves musterers, fishermen, shepherds, prospectors, deer cullers, fire watchers, forestry workers, or lighthouse keepers; but their true title, that of their earliest Polynesian forerunners, is *tangata whenua*—men of the land. Men who, coming to terms with the wilderness, inhabit with ease this land they inherit. Men as native as the kiwi.

> *. . . men of strength*
> *Proved at football and in wars not their own.*
> —ALLEN CURNOW

THE HUMAN KIWI, then. He has climbed Everest first. He has often run the men of other nations into the ground on the Olympic track. He has built boats to jet up rivers where none have gone before. He has split the atom first, sent rockets to Venus.

Of his ruggedness and bravery there is no question. He can be the only fighting soldier to win the Victoria Cross, for valour in action, twice in the twentieth century. That he has proved himself as a warrior his enemies would scarcely dispute. Indeed some historians maintain that New Zealand only came of age as a nation on April 25, 1915, on the bloody beaches and slopes of Gallipoli.

In the first world war New Zealand suffered more casualties, in proportion to population, than any other nation involved; one of every two men sent overseas was killed or wounded. In the second world war Mussolini saw fit to make a radio broadcast warning the Italian people of the horrors in store should the barbarous New Zealanders invade their country; he ignored the British and Americans.

A man of action, then? Yes, but a dreamer too. The thought of the New Zealand that might have been, the New Zealand that might yet be, still haunts the New Zealand imagination. And from this fertile spiritual tension poets have sprouted from the settled acre in quantity and quality sufficient to rival the rest of the English-speaking world. We still calculate everything—sheep, cattle, and poets alike—to the acre in this predominantly pastoral country. Like erratic glow-worms in an unexplored cave, the poets have illumined the dark contours of the Antipodean soul. Following their fitful gleam are the painters, prose writers, and composers.

Outside his country the Kiwi may seem shy, rather reserved; but this is easily explained. People from a frontier society, with little artifice, and even less conceit, go very naked in the world. It's not simply a question of manners; it is also a question of speech. The only words he knows may be too blunt. So he's careful.

And, outside New Zealand, it's possible that you'll only get the Kiwi talking vigorously on one subject—his own country. He may sometimes speak with contempt or distaste, but like a lover talking of an unfaithful mistress. For nostalgia will probably come welling through his speech. New Zealand sends many such into the world, and most return. The human Kiwi, like the bird itself, is not built for exile. He withers internally, grows old too soon. For his tragedy is that he can abandon his country yet not forget it; his country refuses to abandon him. It haunts him, as one poet put it, like a debt unpaid, a love betrayed. As it did Katherine Mansfield, who, after rejecting it, yearned to make her undiscovered country leap into the imagination of the old world.

Yet, on his native earth, he loses his diffidence. Here he is sure of himself; this, after all, is the land he has mastered. He defends it hotly against criticism, resists intrusion, is often suspicious of foreigners. But, underneath, it's still the same Kiwi speaking: a man uncertain of himself, an Adam unsure of his Eden.

On his reverse side, though, he is scarcely afraid of the world outside. This has been proved often enough in peace as well as war. Today you'll find the Kiwi building roads in Borneo, teaching school in Burma, helping feed Indonesia. This secular missionary tradition, this acceptance of responsibility for the pains of the world, is hardly new; in Pacific jungles or on the plains of China the Kiwi has long been known. He has taken the best spirit of his country out to the world, and brought the world home to his country. So that New Zealand changes too, like the returning Kiwi.

The importance of his European ancestry diminishes, and he becomes more and more a citizen of the Pacific. Where, at last, he now knows his country belongs.

For man has not long felt at home here. The Polynesians, even after a thousand or more years, still looked back to their homeland, a place more and more mythical, which they called Hawaiki. The late-coming Europeans also possessed a Hawaiki, a place in the North Sea which in turn became a myth. New Zealanders have been slow to accept that the greatness that was Britain has passed from the world. Yet Britain, even if its imperial day is done, is still spiritually powerful. And few New Zealanders would want to banish the best of their British inheritance: their legal system, for example, or parliamentary democracy.

New Zealand has not simply followed; she has often led the British Commonwealth and the world in social advance. This was the first country in the world to give women the vote, the first to establish an effective social security system. In abolishing capital punishment, New Zealand led both Britain and America. And this is possibly still the world's best-padded welfare state. Despite grim prophecies, young New Zealanders look none the worse for having been brought up in it.

The paradox of the Kiwi is that he is a self-proclaimed individualist who lives in one of the world's most collective societies. In New Zealand it's possible to be rich, but not very rich. It's also possible to be poor, but not very poor. The frontier meant liberty, but it also meant hardship. The pioneer, of necessity, looked towards the infant central government to solve his problems of isolation, and sometimes to fight his battles. Today farmer or city worker still looks to the State in much the same way. Yet the State has not grown into a monster. Bureaucracy is present, but seldom rampant. If a New Zealander has a problem, he can take it direct to the prime minister if he wishes —simply by calling the man on the telephone.

This can in part be explained away by smallness of population. But only in part. Another inheritance from the pioneers is an easy-going attitude towards authority. A prime minister who made himself inaccessible behind secretaries wouldn't last long in New Zealand. "Who does he think *he* is?" would be the cry.

As long ago as 1885 Froude remarked on "a certain republican equality of manners" among the colonists. In this respect, at least, he would find New Zealand unchanged today.

If the republican ideals of the French revolution—liberty, equality, fraternity—were present in New Zealand from the time of the first European settlement, the heaviest emphasis, by far, has been on equality. This has not always meant uniformity. Even in the city, on his quarter-acre section, the Kiwi can still choose to be different from his neighbours if he wishes; he still possesses the freedom of choice he had when the tangled bush was his home. The Kiwi is a curious bird, but seldom intolerant. The right to dissent received its largest test in the 1960s, with the country divided over involvement in the Indo-Chinese war and continued sporting contact with South Africa; in both instances dissent prevailed in the long run. In the 1970s do-it-yourself New Zealanders, dismayed by government inaction about fallout hazard, sailed small protest boats to the French nuclear test area. So New Zealanders can hardly be styled apathetic any longer.

Equality, in New Zealand, has meant equality of opportunity, an instinctive detestation of privilege. The country, after all, was settled by men who declined to bow their heads. The republicans and dreamers, the socialists and liberals, the idealists and utopians, who exported themselves from Europe to the South Pacific a hundred or more years ago, might be perplexed by much of present-day New Zealand. But I doubt if they would be altogether dismayed.

And liberty? If the Kiwi can still think what he likes, say what he likes, that doesn't mean he can expect everyone to stand up and cheer ("Who does he think *he* is?"). On the contrary a man of strongly individual opinion will still be greeted by frontier suspicion of the new. But liberty, in New Zealand, means more than freedom to speak one's mind. It also means freedom from hunger, freedom from poverty, freedom from smog and overcrowding, from the worst features of industrial civilization. The Kiwi possesses a physical freedom unmatched in the world.

Chief ingredients of this physical freedom are bush and mountain, sand and sea. In most towns and cities the wilderness still raps pleasantly on the door; freedom from job or office is never far away. At weekends or on holidays New Zealanders rush in tens of thousands for the empty spaces.

Fairest earth . . .
let us come to you
barefoot, as befits love,
as the boy to the trembling girl,
as the child to the mother:
seeking before all things the honesty of substance,
touch of soil and wind and rock,
frost and flower and water,
the honey of the senses.

—A. R. D. FAIRBURN

NEW ZEALANDERS are nominally a Christian people, but the flavour of the national life is pagan. Particularly is this true of the north of New Zealand, of Auckland and beyond, where the sun is warmer, winters are milder, and the horizon sweeps away unbroken towards the tropical Pacific. For New Zealanders worship sun and nature as few other peoples in the world.

Ours is a nation of yachtsmen and trampers, swimmers and mountain climbers, fishermen and hunters, beachcombers and skiers. Between the salt spray of a wandering coast and the rugged peaks above the snowline, our national life has grown.

But our truly unifying national pastime has its origin far away—at Rugby school in England, where once a confused boy, rather than kick a football, picked it up and ran. Rugby is a game for warriors; and glory attaches itself to those who, in their youth, are selected to wear the national All Black or Kiwi jersey—who go out on a green field to battle fiercely with the Rugby giants of France, England, South Africa, or Australia.

Individualism and teamwork: the paradox is there, not only in our social life but in our recreation too.

Here is the Kiwi, then. Make what you will of him. But don't try to pin him down. He eludes all categories.

> *But now there are no more islands to be found*
> *And the eye scans risky horizons of its own*
> *In unsettled weather, and murmurs of the drowned*
> *Haunt their familiar beaches—*
> *Who navigates us towards what unknown*
> *But not improbable provinces? Who reaches*
> *A future down for us from the high shelf*
> *Of spiritual daring?*
>
> —ALLEN CURNOW

THE NEW ZEALAND that was, the New Zealand that is; what of the New Zealand that will be? Historian and sociologist, politician and poet—all offer confusing answers.

Perhaps only the geographer can be trusted. New Zealand is a new nation of Pacific islanders situated in the south of the South Pacific, between the Asian and American continents. Its people have been slow to reconcile themselves to geography, but such events as the Indo-Chinese war, and Britain's withdrawal from her old outposts in favour of liaison with continental Europe, made the truth vivid in the 1960s, and confirmed the country's growing consciousness of independent nationhood. Trade and diplomatic links have been built on both sides of the Pacific basin; the country is no longer a mere food-basket for Britain. Nor is it simply a white man's stronghold in the South Pacific. Though Asian immigration has been severely and sometimes cruelly restricted since the nineteenth century, with often third-rate European migrants preferred to first-rate Asians, inner racial patterns have begun accelerating change. Within a few generations every New Zealander is likely to have some Polynesian blood. In the early 1970s about one New Zealander in nine or ten was Polynesian; by the end of the century, on present population projections, it could be one in four or five. And this is not to take into account tens of thousands of Europeans who already take pride in Polynesian blood. Though the high Maori birth rate has abated slightly, with increased urbanization of the race, steady migration from present or past tropical Polynesian dependencies means that one *new* New Zealander in five (by birth or migration) is now Polynesian.

In other ways too change is coming fast. Maori language and Polynesian culture are no longer altogether neglected in schools and universities; the country is by degrees becoming truly bicultural as well as biracial. This is emphasized by a growing number of Maori writers and artists who take strength from the twin cultures of the land. And not only Maoris; it is significant, for example, that New Zealand's greatest poet, James K. Baxter (1926–72), took immense strength from Polynesian mythology and Maori tradition towards the end of his short potent life, and called for the Maori virtue of *aroha* (unselfish love) to be embraced by New Zealanders of European descent. When he died, he was buried and mourned as a Maori, by Maori tribesmen.

Already, then, something new is plain; something no one quite counted on. Long blinkered by imported myths, old Hawaikis, the New Zealander has been slow, too slow, to perceive that his nation may have a distinctive destiny in the great family of mankind. And that destiny begins to seem a new Pacific adventure, sprung from a mixture of men building afresh on remote islands.

NEW ZEALAND TODAY is a land which has known hunger and war, hardship and sacrifice. A land which now knows peace and abundance. A land where man nurses and harvests the earth to his need.

But now let the land itself speak—the durable land and its people.

*The cities of
New Zealand—clean,
shining cities of wind and
rain, sun and sea—cities where
the townsman works and earns, buys
and sells, lives and loves, plays and creates. . . .*

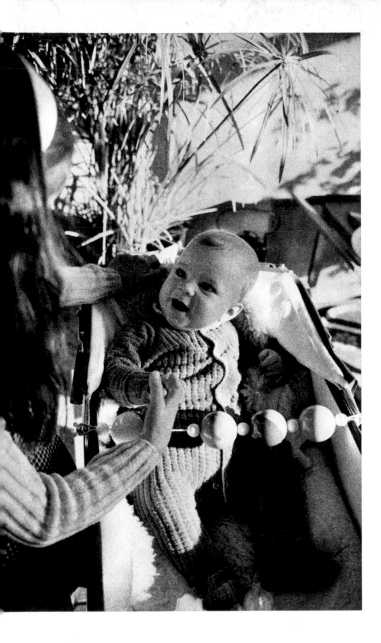

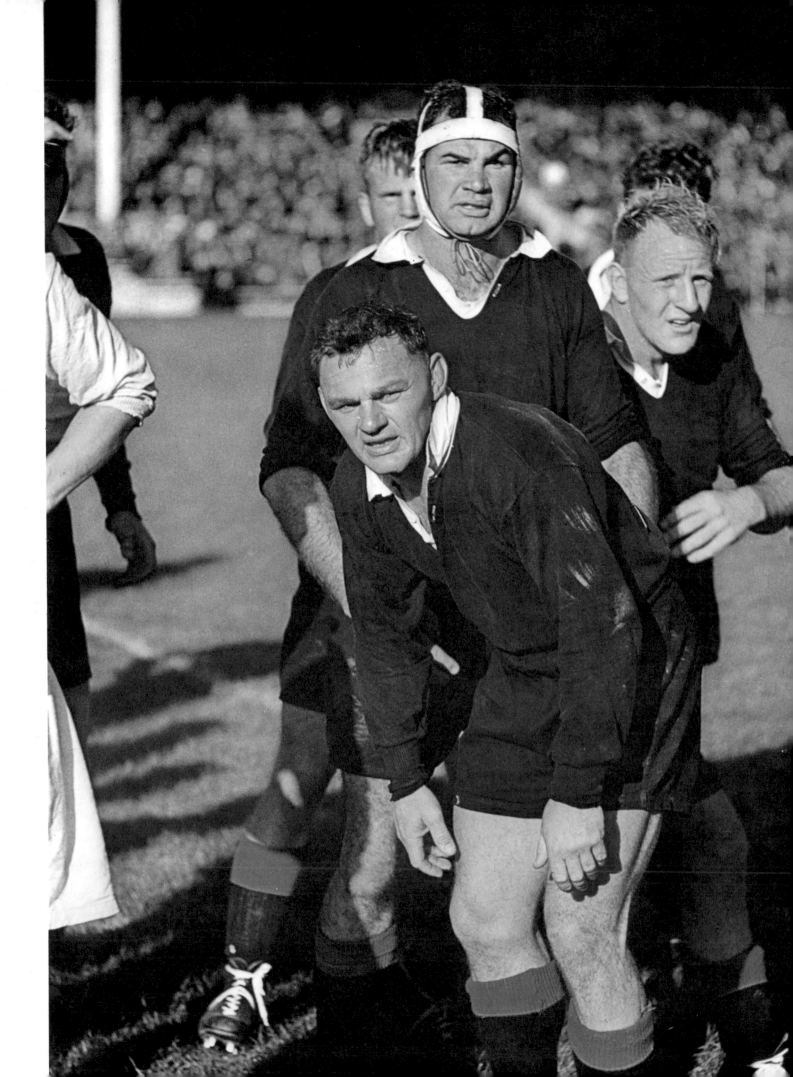

But the cities still depend on the soil the pioneers won . . .

. . . for from soil
comes wealth
for the nation,
food and warmth
for the world.

In this country,
some run herds . . .

. . . others graze sheep . . .

. . . some harvest the rivers . . .

. . . others farm the sea . . .

and all find time for fun. . . .

He stands close to the earth,

My obdurate countryman,

Drawing from the wind's breath,

The arid sweetness of flower and mountain.

—COLIN NEWBURY

When God made this place
He made mountains and fissures
Hostile, vicious, and turned
Away His face . . .

Yet it might be His purpose to plant
The immaculate metal
Where the stoutest hearts quail.

—DENIS GLOVER

BETWEEN PLAIN AND peak is the high country. Starkly sculptured by wind, weather, and the convulsions of time, this empty rugged upland, where only the toughest vegetation grows, hardly welcomes men.

The Polynesian had no use for it. Fresh from the tropics, he would have felt alien here. In winter, blizzards roar down the valleys, whitening the tussock. In summer, the sun can roast; but the nights are always cooling.

This is a land of strange, primeval beauties. Of tussock which grows luminous at sunset. Of delicate flowers the colour of frost. Of avalanches and shingle slides and tumbling, booming water. It is a place where, from rock and light, the lonely imagination can conjure eerie visions; a landscape terrible and complete in itself, where man will always remain a tiny intruder.

A bleak land, an angry land; yet a land where everything is space and light. The space and sweep of a continent. The dazzling light of the world's greatest ocean. This is the South Island's high country.

THE FIRST SETTLERS rushed for these empty spaces. First they hunted gold, then they grazed sheep. For sheep, if not men, could find the climate tolerable. Sheep could flourish, roaming tussock country, their wool ample protection against frost and snow.

So men drove their thin flocks up into the high valleys where rivers, in sprawling stony beds, find a dozen winding channels; where cold and lonely lakes mirror only mountain and sky. The sheep were set loose in this emptiness. And, as their flocks wandered, the men built themselves homesteads on lower, warmer ground. Around them, for shelter and reassurance, they planted the shedding trees of Europe—trees which, in autumn, add an unexpected colour to remote places beneath the mountains. Many of these homesteads still stand today.

To the high country in 1860 came a young Englishman named Samuel Butler. On a sheep run at the headwaters of the Rangitata River he brooded on the mountains around him. And from this meditation came the opening chapters of a novel which the world knows today as *Erewhon*. "Never," he wrote, "shall I forget the utter loneliness of the prospect . . . the vastness of mountain and plain, river and sky. . . ."

TODAY, THE SHEEP must still be mustered much as they were a century ago. In autumn they are brought down to the winter country, to the lower ground where they will not be buried by snow. In spring, as the snow flees up the mountains, they are shorn, and the mobs flow back up the valleys, grazing wherever vegetation is to be found.

Each autumn the musterers and their dogs have the toughest job in New Zealand. In the hectic days of the muster, when every hour is likely to count because of changing weather, they may scramble three thousand feet over shingle slides, around waterfalls, in pursuit of only two or three sheep. Yet chilled by wind, soaked by rain, half-frozen by snow, these men can still crack jokes at day's end. They pride themselves on their toughness; they make hobbyist mountaineers look foolish. But they are not blind to the dramatic beauty of their surroundings. Familiarity, in the high country, does not breed contempt. I have seen musterers, with all of a lifetime given to the mountains, draw breath and gaze with wonder upon patterns of cloud and rock. And pause wearily in the middle of a muster to pick some alpine flower to decorate a battered hat.

Upon the upland road
Ride easy, stranger:
Surrender to the sky
Your heart of anger.

—JAMES K. BAXTER

In the early morning the muster begins. . . .

. . . From high peaks and steep rock faces the sheep are moved down. . . .

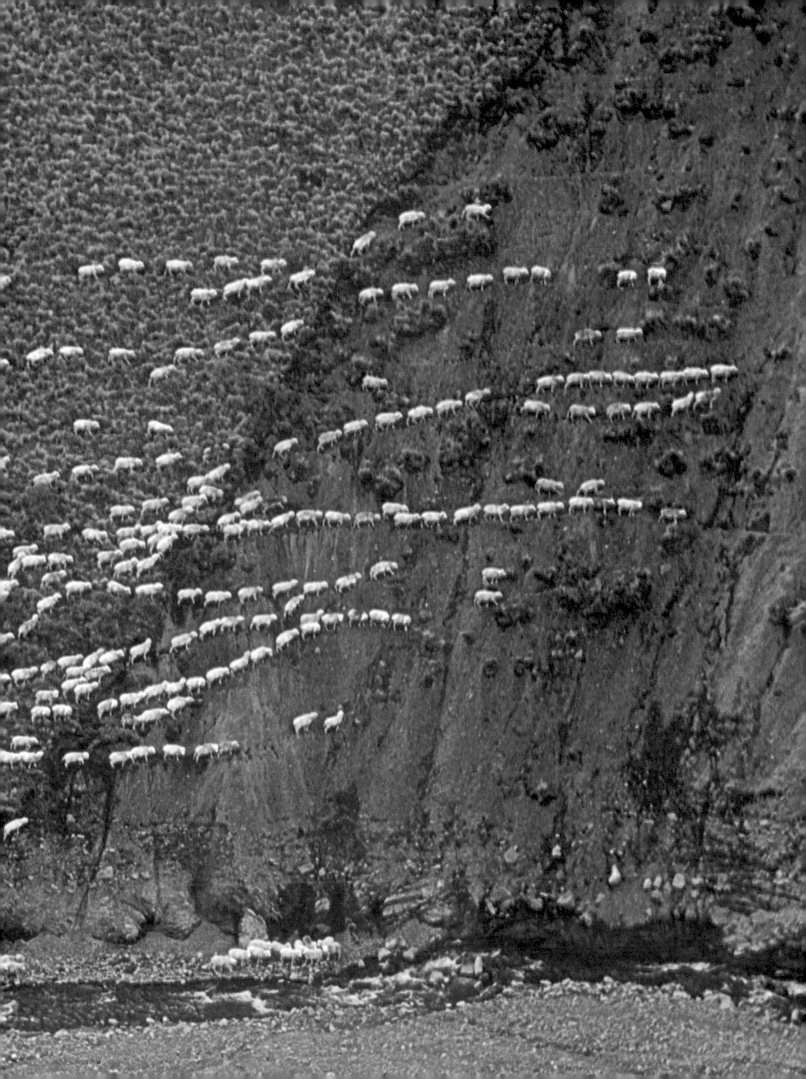

. . . Slowly the mob swells.

Tens become thousands.

And the muster is almost over. . . .

Postscript, 1973

> *Is there a kowhai in the blood,*
> *When all the trees are in the park, and dead?*
> *. . . There is a kowhai in the blood,*
> *Which knows no autumn where it thrives,*
> *An image in the garden we design,*
> *And live with our reality inside.*
>
> —KEITH SINCLAIR

NEW ZEALAND isn't easy to trap in a typewriter—or, for that matter, on film or canvas. For a dozen years I've been fashioning phrases, in books and articles, to explain what it's like to know this country as a lover. And trying to claim it as my own. But never very satisfyingly. Perhaps love affairs should be left alone. Because most of what I've written falls far short of what I feel, and thus far short of the truth. And yet here I am, trying again, a curious contest. These pages will perish. This land will live. Human beings can't claim it. The land claims them.

Perhaps the best way to see New Zealand, in the end, is as a land which the human race almost forgot. Convert the time of man upon this planet to twenty-four hours, and human occupancy of these islands becomes only a minute or two. There are no overgrown ruins to haunt the historian; the mysteries of the human past are slender. The land—of high mountains, wild shores and lonely places—is easier to celebrate than man's often brutally intrusive presence here. As a country New Zealand has vivid character; as a man the New Zealander is still shaping his character upon the obstinate anvil of the land.

It has seldom been a pleasant sight. Forested hills turned to eroded desert. Characterless towns and suburbs haphazardly planted where bulldozers have done their worst. Power pylons, as insensitively placed as graffiti upon a shrine, stalking across scenes of vast aboriginal beauty. Roads and railways lacerating forest and coast. It all tells of a century's violent growth and huge endeavour. New Zealanders, in their haste to harness the land, have often had a spectacularly cruel way of imposing themselves upon the natural world.

But that's not all there is to be said. The country is still far from swamped with human handiwork. There are remarkably many places which have survived man's onslaught, some of the most concentrated and spectacular wilderness left intact in the world. There are seascapes as pristine and dramatic as the day they were first sighted by Polynesian and European voyagers. Mountains have always been obstacles to progress; they rise serene and undiminished above the plains. There are quiet fiords which echo only with the sound of willowy waterfalls, lost harbours and long gull-haunted beaches, deep valleys rich with rioting bush which man can never plunder. And places where the old pagan mystery of the earth lingers in the air like the slow blue smoke of a campfire.

It's still possible to find loneliness in this land. The kind of loneliness which goes back to long before the time of lonely crowds and urban jungles. The old, original loneliness: that of Adam in the Garden. Or that of the first man to walk with wonder, fashioning symbols and legends to explain himself in his world.

Elsewhere there are places, backwaters, which man has largely abandoned; and which have their own vivid appeal. Places like Northland, Westland, Central Otago, which man once ransacked for native treasure—timber, gum, gold. Here the tranquillity of remote islands reasserts itself. Man has left the battlefield strewn with relics of his feverish tenure. Wounds have healed, towns have fallen back into returning bush while beaches heap with whitening driftwood; under the disorderly vegetation, the earth collects its fragmented memory. The landscape comes to terms with the few men who remain, and men with the landscape; often there is a pleasant truce declared. In such places the present is still the frontier past. Man has not always left ugliness. Sometimes the beauty bequeathed is stark: in the north stately homesteads, built from the timber of the great kauri which brought men here, founder gently among fern and dark Monterey pine. Sometimes it is delicate: to the rocky hillsides and river flats of Central Otago were brought the deciduous trees of Europe and North America, which light valleys with trembling, alien colour in autumn. There is a residual richness in the aftermath of man's first encounter with the land.

There is also time, perhaps, for man to consider his business here. The kind of life he would most like to live; the kind of country he would most like his children to inherit. The voyagers of Polynesia and the voyagers of Europe meet in the modern New Zealander, a man who thinks he knows the good life when he sees it, and is no longer so inclined to bargain away his birthright for easy dollars. For that is the message which can be read in New Zealand's recent history. When environmental concern began to mount in the Western World in the late 1960s, nowhere did the tide flow stronger than in this small South Pacific country. New Zealanders had at last begun to feel that they had put too much of their pristine landscape—lakes, forests, rivers, beaches—on the line in the interest of greater gross national product. The crunch came with the proposed sacrifice of luminous Lake Manapouri, in the South Island, for hydro power to serve an aluminium industry. The lake fast became a symbol of the conservationist cause—it stood for all that man was likely to lose in his pursuit of quick profit. And all the aluminium in the world, it seemed, wouldn't compensate New Zealanders for the massacre of Manapouri. Even in briskly commercial Auckland city, 600 miles north, where most have never seen the lake, car stickers flashed the plea: SAVE MANAPOURI. Aucklanders, though, were possibly thinking as much of the last scattered stands of the once vast kauri forest still under savage attack.

So enough was enough, and New Zealanders were to say so with their votes in 1972. For the first time in the Western World, environment became a vital—and in places decisive—issue in a national election campaign. And those politicians who underestimated the feeling of the New Zealander for his land paid the penalty.

Yet that feeling had long been evident, for anyone to see, in the country's creative culture. The New Zealander's delight in the contours of his country has been an obsessional element in his literature and art, ever since a truly native accent in our culture became apparent. That delight, indeed, largely makes our creative culture individual and vivid among that of other nations—witness the best work of our poets, novelists and painters. The land has often been as central to their vision as it was to the myth-makers of the Maori who graced landscapes with some of the most haunting legends to which mankind is heir, and everywhere left place-names of poetic power. The country's most resonant poet, James K. Baxter, saw in New Zealand 'the face of a primeval goddess, pitted by the sun, by earthquake, and waves of the sea'. The country's most vigorous modern painter, Colin McCahon, has expressed his aspiration thus: 'I saw something logical, orderly and beautiful belonging to the land and not yet to its people.' Such remarkable individuals have sharpened sensitivity around them, offering fresh delight in the land they celebrate. Perhaps it was no great wonder, then, that the New Zealander should have used his vote so vehemently.

Now that this antipodean Adam has sprung to defence of his Eden, the question is whether he is prepared to pay the price to preserve it—to sacrifice a little affluence, to become less a consumer, and to accept that the native quality of life in these islands *is* part of his standard of living, something not measurable in dollars and cents. If he does so with good grace, then he will be the first Westerner to turn from the treadmills and illusory rewards of societies geared to conspicuous consumption with reckless disregard of the planet's diminishing resources and vanishing splendours. Yet the first step has been taken. New Zealanders will soon learn whether they can live comfortably with the consequences of their choice. And for the land itself there is at least a breathing space, a reprieve. It may yet glow green and lonely in a world increasingly blackened by industry, left lifeless by pollution.

So there is now ever more reason for native or visitor to treasure his pleasures in this country's character. To gaze with fresh surprise upon the ocean surging against dramatic and legendary Cape Reinga, the vast bright sands of Ninety Mile Beach, upon the ancient kauri of the Waipoua forest, the crystalline coves of the Bay of Islands. Or to drink deeply from the greens of the Urewera wilderness, the bright skies of Taranaki, the serene shores of the Bay of Plenty, the ferny valleys of the King Country. Or to marvel at the marching mountains of the Maori, where the earth still rumbles, while he warms himself in the waters of the volcanic plateau. Or to enter the starker beauties and huge silences of the South Island, where mountains mass on every skyline and pale daisies glint on tawny tussock foothills. Or wonder at the tranquil tides of the Marlborough Sounds, the lakes and quiet coast of Nelson, the glaciers plunging down to the tangled trees of the verdant West Coast, the canyons and rivers of Otago.

Then in the far south, where forest and fiord seem one in some first dream of creation, perhaps he can pause beside Lake Manapouri, with its silvery waters brimming beneath snow-tipped peaks, where a nation-making legend has lately been born. There he may see that, whatever happens to the rest of the world, much of New Zealand may yet still live as man first found it. This might be the greatest wonder this country can offer the observer. The vision, that is, of a land with such claim on man's affection that it hasn't yet lost its primeval heart, its native soul.

Few islands, after all, have not been adventures for the human spirit. And no islands can have been more obdurate in their strength, so taming the restless tamer that one of our poets, Charles Brasch, can say:

> *Man must lie with the gaunt hills like a lover*
> *Earning their intimacy in the calm sigh*
> *Of a century of quiet and assiduity*
> *Discovering what solitude has meant*
> *Before our headlong time broke upon these waters.*

For this land is still the home of warrior and poet. A land which man may have claimed physically—but which for a second time has itself claimed *him* in spirit.

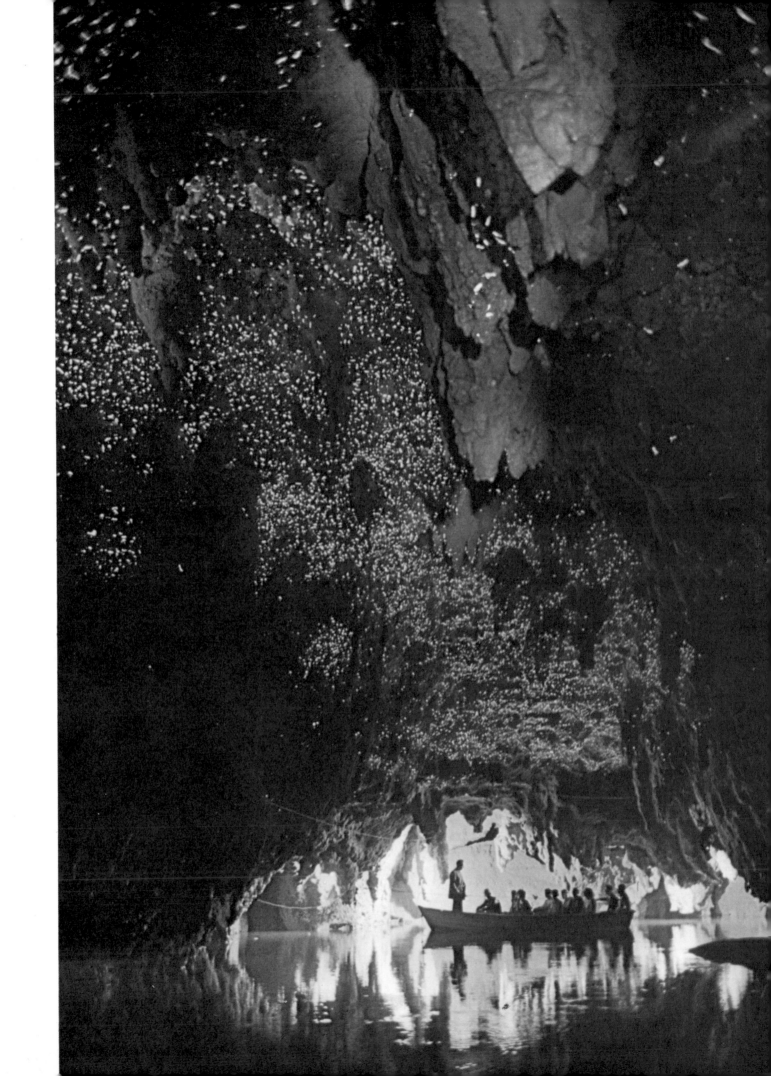

*A horizon that knew Polynesian canoe and European sail—
here, where New Zealand ends and the world begins,
a new race of islanders stands with a wonder-
ing, sometimes troubled, seaward gaze.*

COMMENTARIES ON THE PHOTOGRAPHS

END PAPERS. An impressionistic, early-morning photograph of mountains reflected in the waters of Milford Sound.

TITLE-PAGE SPREAD. View of the South Pacific photographed while flying near White Island in the Bay of Plenty. This bay was so named by Captain Cook in 1769 because he was successful in gathering ample provisions from the Maoris along its coast.

9. Cape Reinga, at the northernmost tip of New Zealand. According to Maori traditions, this is the place where spirits of the dead depart from the country, leaping from the lonely pohutukawa tree near the end of the cape and travelling by way of the underworld to the Polynesians' lost homeland, the legendary Hawaiki.

10–11. About twelve miles by road from the popular Fox Glacier tourist resort in the South Island, Gillespies Beach was formerly an active gold-mining area. It is typical of the lonely beaches along the west coast and provides a fine view of the Alps. It was from off this coast that Tasman first sighted New Zealand and saw the Southern Alps towering over the land.

12–13. An aerial photograph of sunset clouds hanging over the coast of Westland, South Island, near Franz Josef Glacier, with the Southern Alps towering in the distance. The view is southward.

14–15. An early-morning aerial view of the entrance to Milford Sound with a naval ship visible. Milford Sound is the most spectacular of the many fiords that indent the southwestern coastline of the South Island. It is said to have been given its name in the 1820s by whalers, the first Europeans to arrive here, because of a fancied resemblance to Milford Haven in Wales. A true fiord, with an entrance shallower than its headwaters, it was once the bed of a mighty glacier. Even in the days before a tunnel was dug from the head of the Eglinton valley to provide easy access, when the sound could only be approached by sea or a three-day overland trek, the breathtaking scenic beauty of the spot had made it famed throughout the world; earlier still, the Maoris had made expeditions here to gather the tear-drop type of greenstone which they prized so highly.

16–17. It is the punga, or tree fern, growing so abundantly throughout most of both islands, that gives the New Zealand bush its characteristic subtropical appearance. Appropriately, then, it has been adopted as the national emblem of New Zealand and, in stylized forms based on Maori rafter patterns, also provides the motif for the present book, as seen on pages 7, 58, and elsewhere.

18–19. A high-country homestead in the Rakaia valley, South Island, the heart of the sheep-grazing tussock land of Canterbury province. Even today, this area is frequently completely cut off by swollen rivers and washed-out roads, and some local farmers now keep small planes with which to bring in supplies.

20–21. A country church and cabbage tree near Taihape in central North Island. Originally a sawmilling and railway-construction base, this area was populated by settlers from Christchurch in the 1890s and, with the clearing of the bush, has become good pastoral land.

22. A dead tree left behind after a bush fire. Scenes such as this are typical of many areas in New Zealand where the first settlers burnt the bush to make fast money in sheep and cattle grazing. This has caused serious problems in land erosion in many areas. In recent years, however, much of the land has been improved and brought back into use by re-afforestation and by aerial top-dressing.

23. Rich dairy lands beneath Mt. Egmont, near New Plymouth, Taranaki province, North Island. An extinct volcano with a height of 8,260 feet, Mt. Egmont is called Taranaki by the Maoris, perhaps meaning the "gliding peak". According to Maori legend, Taranaki once stood near two other volcanoes in central North Island, Ruapehu and Ngauruhoe, but was banished to the far west after a domestic quarrel with them. As he went, he made the great mark in the earth that is now filled with the Wanganui River. One day, it is said, Taranaki will be forgiven and permitted to return to his original position, and there are still said to be Maoris who fear to live along the path the mountain will use on this return journey.

24. The Canterbury Plains, with Christchurch as their population centre, are an alluvial area formed by the many rivers flowing out of the Southern Alps and contain some of the country's richest farmlands. First settled in 1850 by Church of England colonists,

Christchurch was the scene of the final colonization project of the New Zealand Company before it surrendered its charter to the Crown.

33. Near the entrance to Mangonui Harbour, on Doubtless Bay near the northern tip of Northland peninsula. Mud flats such as these, often thick with mangroves, are a feature of Northland's labyrinthine harbours, where the tides ebb and flow with great swiftness.

34–35. Waipu Cove. An attractive part of Northland's much-indented and pohutukawa-laced eastern coastline. The Waipu area was settled in the 1850s by six boatloads of Scottish evangelical pilgrims who came by way of a short-lived community in Nova Scotia, under leadership of stern patriarchal Norman McLeod.

36–37. In the southern part of South Island's Westland, near Franz Josef Glacier, lies beautiful Lake Mapourika, bordered by dense rain forest and noted for its reflections of both trees and mountains. From this region, once familiar to Maoris in search of greenstone, comes the kotuku, or rare white heron, which according to legend is seen but once in a lifetime.

38. Pohutu Geyser, at the Maori village of Whakarewarewa, near Rotorua on the North Island's central plateau, is the most spectacular geyser in this active thermal region. The Rotorua region is famed for its scenery, its thermal activity, and the medicinal qualities of its water. It is the home of the Arawa tribe and of many of the most attractive Maori legends.

40. A carved figure outside the model Maori village, or pa, of Whakarewarewa at Rotorua. The Maori race is renowned for its superb wood carving, of which this is an interesting example. The sticks in the foreground form part of the typical palisade that guards a pa.

41. A young Maori girl at a celebration held in the Maori settlement of Turangawaewae at Ngaruawahia in the valley of the Waikato River. Turangawaewae is the seat of the present king of the tribe, Koroki, and the scene of many Maori ceremonies and celebrations. Situated some seventy-four miles south of Auckland, Ngaruawahia is the centre of a rich dairy and farming region.

42–43. More Maoris at the same celebration at Ngaruawahia (see preceding commentary). The old woman is one of the few who still bear the *moko,* or tattoo. Formerly tattooing was very common, and tribal chiefs were identified by the distinctive patterns of their *moko,* which often covered their faces and much of their bodies. For example, many of the signers of the Treaty of Waitangi (see page 57) drew simplified patterns from their facial tattoos rather than sign an X after their names. Another of the photographs shows how Maoris love to sit and talk about both the past and the present; the group seen here might be discussing their fancies for next Saturday's race meeting or the famous canoe of a remote ancestor.

44–45. A gathering of returned servicemen discussing their problems within the Maori community at the Waitangi Maori meetinghouse. Waitangi, located on the Bay of Islands, Northland, is the historic site of the signing of the treaty that bears its name (see page 57). Beside the restored Treaty House is this beautiful example of the Maori meetinghouse, which contains outstanding works of Maori art.

46. School children learning of the Maori and Pacific past at Auckland's War Memorial Museum. Schools in the main cities regularly take their pupils to the local museums for lectures.

47. Students at Hillary College (named for New Zealand's Everest conqueror) in Auckland's southern suburbs. Enrolment of 1,000 is nearly sixty per cent Maori and other Polynesians, reflecting the recent urbanization of the Polynesian. School has Polynesian studies, Polynesian club with white students involved, also teaches Maori and Samoan languages.

48. Maori students at Kaitaia College, Northland.

49. Students and master carver teacher at Maori arts and crafts school in Rotorua's thermal area, Whakarewarewa. This modern building, like the industry within, reflects cultural resurgence of the Maori race.

50. A Maori orator in flax skirt and kiwi-feather cloak at the annual Waitangi Treaty celebration (see page 57). This treaty, besides being a landmark in New Zealand history, also marks the first time in

the history of British colonization that the natives of a country were approached as landowners with rights of their own. The anniversary of its signing on February 6, 1840, is always marked with fitting ceremonies.

51. Scenes from annual Ngaruawahia Regatta, now a largely Maori-run event, in which canoe-racing and hurdling feature; the day brings thousands of Maoris and Europeans together from all over Waikato and Auckland areas.

52–53. Maori pupils at Hillary College, South Auckland; Maori girl performing at Ngaruawahia Regatta; Maori workers in Vulcan Lane Auckland.

54–55. Maori women at the Ngaruawahia Regatta.

56. Maori sailors at the Waitangi Treaty celebration (see commentary for page 50). One is holding the *taiaha,* an early weapon now used ceremonially when making a speech or giving a challenge.

69. Sunbathers at Oriental Bay, Wellington. This warm sand is only a few hundred yards from the busy streets of New Zealand's capital and principal harbour. Named after the famed "Iron Duke", Wellington was settled in 1840, just before New Zealand was proclaimed a British colony.

70–71. Wellington, capital of New Zealand, home of Parliament, politicians and a thousand government offices, with skyline fast soaring higher on limited level ground. Elsewhere houses climb skyward up steep hillsides. With urban population approaching 350,000, exposed Wellington takes gales from the turbulent Cook Strait, which separates North and South Islands. Now a community of some sophistication, with diplomats a cosmopolitan leaven, Wellington also has reasonably bracing cultural climate.

72–73. New Zealanders; A youngster, wet-haired from his morning dip, starts a hearty New Zealand meal. With a long history of planned babycare New Zealanders pride themselves on a healthy youthful nation. In this country the population is reputed to buy more books per head than any other English-speaking nation. In the north of North Island, homes are planned for the temperate, nearly subtropical climate and enjoy wide sweeps of sea, distant headlands or green, rolling landscape.

74–75. Dunedin scenes. Uniquely and preciously flavoured with its past, a treasurehouse of Victoriana in the South Seas, Dunedin was settled in 1848 by hardy Scots voyagers in landscape not unlike that which they left behind. Centrepiece of the city (right) is statue of bard Robert Burns, whose puritan nephew was one of Dunedin's founders. Gold rushes made Dunedin wealthy and early home for much New Zealand commercial enterprise. When capital began to go elsewhere, Dunedin settled and made very pleasant best of itself, strongly coloured by its university and large student population. An amiable and leisurely place, with fairly static population of 112,000, Dunedin has wild open country within minutes of centre.

75 (right). Spectators at the Riccarton racecourse, Christchurch.

76. Saturday cricket matches on the Domain are a typical part of the Auckland scene. On the hill in the background is the War Memorial Museum.

77. Rugby is without doubt New Zealand's favourite national sport. Here an All Blacks trial match is being held at Wellington's Athletic Park.

78–79. The NZBC (or National) Symphony Orchestra at rehearsal and at concert in the Wellington Town Hall, with guests Vladimir Ashkenasy and Lili Kraus. The orchestra, after brave beginnings in 1940s, is now potent force in New Zealand cultural life, and held in high regard internationally.

The artists and craftsmen have always striven for a New Zealand identity and in the last decade there has been a conscious and vital development. (Left to right) Rei Hamon, a North Island bushman turned artist in 1968 after a serious back injury teaching himself to draw with pen and ink in a style that depicts his love for detail and intimate knowledge of the New Zealand bush. Doreen Blumhardt's energy and enthusiasm is characteristic of the New Zealand potter. Her efforts, along with those of many others, have helped this craft become a by-word of New Zealand's cultural attainments. John Drawbridge, one of New Zealand's foremost painters and engravers, whose work is widely acclaimed in his homeland and abroad. His prints hang in a number of permanent collections around the world, among them The Victoria and Albert Museum and the British Museum. Guy Ngan, a New Zealand-born Chinese, whose profession is architecture but whose chosen forms of expression are print making, painting and sculpture. His works in cast metals create a frontispiece to many a modern New Zealand building.

80–81. Auckland city looking south from North Shore. With urban population of 700,000, by far New Zealand's largest city, unplanned Auckland has now swamped all available ground on the isthmus, spotted with extinct volcanoes, between harbours of Waitemata (pictured) and Manukau (in distance) and is still fast spreading north, west and south. Almost one New Zealander in four is an Aucklander; a third of country's trade passes across wharves. Once New Zealand's frontier capital, Auckland now has fair claim to be Polynesia's capital (more than twenty languages spoken) as well as business and more recently cultural capital of country. Most boisterous and urgent urban climate in New Zealand.

82–83. Christchurch scenes featuring new town hall, which has become cultural landmark for all New Zealand both in architectural form and in the activity it is so brilliantly designed to house—New Zealand's sober answer to Sydney's Opera House. Quite splendid but unostentatious on lovely riverside site, the building makes the 280,000 hearts of Christchurch citizenry beat faster with pride—this in a city wonderfully flavoured with Victorian Gothic architecture, among lavish gardens laid down by visionary English pioneers of nineteenth century, which until now has had cathedral as apex. Designed by Christchurch architects Miles Warren and Maurice Mahoney, town hall has main auditorium seating nearly 2,700, with space for choir of 400 and orchestra of 100; secondary auditorium for drama seats 1,200 amid complex also containing bars, conference halls, coffee bar and waterside restaurant.

84 (top). A dairy herd passes an abandoned pioneer building near Waihi, on the Pacific coast southeast of Auckland. Waihi was the site of the discovery in 1878 of the famed Martha Hill gold and silver lode, and is now a thriving farming and light industrial area.

84 (bottom). Aerial top-dressing of pastureland near the North Island's Kaingaroa pine forest, Rotorua. The country's agricultural production has been greatly boosted by such examples of New Zealand ingenuity. The Kaingaroa pine forest, the biggest man-made forest in the world, is now being harvested for paper pulp and timber exports.

85. Boys exhibiting a calf at Dunedin's annual Agricultural and Pastoral Show. Shows such as this are held throughout the country and play a prominent part in New Zealand's rural life. The "A & P Show" is a focal point during the year for each locality.

86–87. Representative of the living standards, which have always been high in New Zealand, these four photographs show continuing upward growth. A housing complex under construction on Auckland's North Shore. Butter from Auckland's cool stores being loaded onto ships for export to Europe and more recently Asia, a growing market. A wool store in Christchurch and a super-market in Auckland.

88–89. Dairy farmers at the A & P Show in Kumeu, near Auckland.

90. A high-country sheep farmer at his property near the road from Christchurch to Arthur's Pass and Westland.

91. A high-country farmer at a sheep sale held yearly at Lake Tekapo, Mackenzie Country, South Island. Mackenzie, after whom the county is named, was a colourful figure in the area's pioneering past; he discovered this high plateau and used it to hide the sheep he would steal from runs further north, drive over unexplored country, and sell to farmers in the south.

92–93. Big Bay, near Milford Sound on the southwest coast of the South Island, makes a lonely home for fishermen during the whitebait season. Small planes from Queenstown on Lake Wakatipu fly in to land on the hard sand beach and collect the tinned whitebait.

94–95. Fishermen amateur and professional. Scene right is in Russell hotel, once a roaring grog-shop in days when village was known as hell-hole of South Pacific—home, according to Charles Darwin in 1835, of 'the very refuse of society'. Carousing seamen, deserters, escaped convicts from Australia camped here amid Maoris—to despair of missionaries intent on saving Polynesian souls. Today a prospering if quiet tourist trap, especially for big-game fishermen seeking swordfish and marlin and mako, richly flavoured with nineteenth-century landmarks.

96. Wood-chopping is always a prominent feature of agricultural and pastoral shows in New Zealand, with axemen demonstrating often stunning strength and skills.

97. Pianist at a country dance at Ross, in Westland. Once an important gold-mining centre, today Ross is mainly a farming and sawmilling community.

98. A Polynesian club performing at a lunch-time concert in the Wellington University. With the influx of islanders from the Pacific these groups are becoming increasingly popular. An Auckland shoe factory worker. New Zealand encourages the establishment of such secondary manufacture and is becoming known for its quality products.

99. Long hair has arrived and New Zealand youth have taken the fashion for their own. In some schools hair-nets are the order of the day in engineering classes. Wellington University, along with all higher educational establishments in New Zealand, accept students from many Asian lands. This has led to a greater understanding of New Zealand's future position as part of Asia.

100. Young countryman at agricultural show.

105–12. Scenes from a sheep muster on Mt. Possession in the South Island's Canterbury province. These are the musterers of the Mt. Possession Run Company, a typical high-country station which takes in more than 100,000 acres of river, plain, and mountain, and grazes 25,000 sheep.

117. Glow-worm Grotto, Waitomo Cave, near Hamilton. The Waitomo Caves, of which this is the principal one, are one of the many features of the craggy limestone country in central North Island known as the King Country. This is where tribes supporting the Maori king fled after the bloodshed of the Maori wars. For years afterwards it was forbidden territory to the white man. Waitomo's strange caverns receive visitors from many parts of the world. Glow-worms are the larvae of a small insect that when mature resembles a mosquito. The larvae move about slightly in their webs, attached to the cavern walls, and emit a steady glow.

118. The kauri tree (*Agathis australis*) is found in upper North Island, where giant kauri forests were plundered by the early European settlers for the prized wood; fortunately many trees still remain in national parks and reserves. The tree often attains a height of some eighty feet before branching, and from its wood the Maoris made their huge canoes. The semi-petrified resin of the tree, resembling amber, was once widely gathered for the making of certain kinds of varnish.

119. Milford Sound photographed from above the Bowen Falls, with Mitre Peak in the distance. The light plane is one tourists can hire to bring them from Queenstown to a small air strip near the Milford Sound Hotel.

120. Skiers who have flown from the Hermitage resort hotel near Mt. Cook on the eastern slopes of the Southern Alps to ski on the névé of the Fox Glacier, which originates at the main divide of the Alps, is nine miles long and descends at a rate of a thousand feet a mile. There are hot springs beside the river that emerges from beneath the glacier.

121. Surfer taking wave at Waipu Cove, Northland, with Whangarei heads prominent in background. Surfing began to boom in popularity in the 1960s, and has now, especially in north, become a year-round New Zealand pastime with wet suits to cheat winter's chill. Waipu is one of hundreds of playgrounds sought when surf is up.

122. Yachting on Auckland's Waitemata harbour, where this popular sport flourishes; small craft swarm across harbour and among islands of Hauraki Gulf with first warm breath of spring.

123. Young walkers on the hills overlooking Piha beach, a west coast resort 25 miles from Auckland. Its magnificently rugged and forested shore is popular with surfers and trampers.

124. Beach near Waihi, in the Bay of Plenty. Waihi was once an important gold-mining centre. Millions of pounds worth of gold and silver have been taken from its mines, which are behind and even directly under the present town, since the lode was discovered by McCombie and Lee in 1878.

125. Old gold-miners' cottages at Arrowtown, Central Otago, in the South Island. Once a booming

The "weathermark" identifies this edition as having been designed & produced by John Weatherhill, Inc., 7-6-13 Roppongi, Minato-ku, Tokyo, Japan | Book design & typography by Meredith Weatherby | Layout of photographs by Brian Brake | Colour plates engraved & printed by Dai Nippon Printing Co. | Gravure plates engraved & printed by Nissha | Composition & letterpress printing by Kenkyusha | Binding by Okamoto Bindery.

The main text is set in Monotype Baskerville 12 point, the display lines in hand-set Bulmer italic 18 and 24 point, and the commentaries in Monotype Baskerville 11 point. Bound in unbleached Hakko sailcloth.

gold-mining centre—the original discoverers of gold in the Arrow River are said to have taken more than two hundred pounds in the first few weeks—today Arrowtown is a quiet rural community with a population of fewer than two hundred. The surrounding countryside is noted for its rugged beauty and its brilliant autumn foliage.

126–27. Tikitere, near Rotorua, Auckland province, is a small area of great thermal activity, with pools of boiling mud and ground that is hot to the feet. The name is said to derive from an incident in which a young Maori bride, feeling herself unloved, cast herself into one of the boiling pools, and her parents lamented, saying: "Taku tiki e tere nei" ("Alas, our beloved daughter has floated away"). The locality is sometimes known as Hell's Gate.

128–29. Sunrise over Mangonui Harbour, on Doubtless Bay, Northland. The name is said to mean "plenty of sharks".

130–31. Dart River, fed by glaciers of the Southern Alps, flows into beautiful Lake Wakatipu. This shot shows a jet boat, invented and built in New Zealand, speeding down the river toward the lake. Jet boats such as these, drawing just a few inches of water, have made it possible to travel great distances by lakes and rivers in only a few hours, distances that used to take days by foot or on horseback.

132–33. Autumn at Glendhu Bay, Lake Wanaka, Central Otago. Toward the right of the photograph is Mt. Aspiring, 9,975 feet in height. This is the first view mountaineers get of this beautiful mountain when they are driving up from the plains towards the end of the road. They do not see the summit again until after a day's walk up the valley to the Aspiring Hut. Glendhu Bay is a popular holiday camping spot. The lake, which occupies the bed of an ancient glacier, is thirty miles long and about four miles wide. The entire region is one of surpassing scenic beauty.

134–35. The summit of Mt. Cook, near the coast of the Tasman Sea in central South Island, rises to a height of 12,349 feet, making it the highest mountain in New Zealand. Its Maori name is Aorangi—"Cloud Piercer". First climbed in 1894, it attracts climbers from all over the world. Its glaciers provide excellent skiing and there are many huts in the area. Now light ski-planes fly both climbers and skiers into the area to save much arduous walking; they also drop food to the huts. Note the tiny figures of climbers at the very peak of the mountain. It is interesting to recall that the permanent snow line in New Zealand is quite low and that ice conditions are within easy reach, whereas similar conditions are found only above nineteen thousand feet in, say, the Himalayas. The Tasman Glacier in the background of this photograph is eighteen miles long and varies in width from nine to about two miles, making it one of the great glaciers of the temperate zones; the ice moves from nine to eighteen inches each day. The photograph at the right was taken with a telephoto lens from the Tasman valley near Lake Pukaki; in the foreground is a shed on a high-country sheep station.

136–37. Névé and icefall of the Franz Josef Glacier, with the Tasman Sea in the distance. The glacier is eight miles long, descending to seven hundred feet above sea level and to within only fifteen miles of the coastline, with sub-tropical bush along its lower reaches. At the base of the glacier is located the little town of Waiho, which literally means "smoky waters"— so called possibly because the waters of the Waiho River as they emerge from the glacier look smoky-blue because of the glacier dust.

138–39. Waipu Cove, Northland.

140. Here we return to Cape Reinga, the point at which we began (see page 9), in a sunset view showing dead pohutukawa trees silhouetted against the Pacific Ocean.

LIST OF PHOTOGRAPHS

(Page numbers are used as reference numerals.)

ACKNOWLEDGMENTS

The authors and the publishers wish to thank the following for permission to quote from copyright work: the Oxford University Press for lines from Allen Curnow's *A Small Room with Large Windows* and James K. Baxter's *In Fires of No Return;* the New Zealand University Press for lines from A. R. D. Fairburn's "Dominion" in *Three Poems;* the Caxton Press for lines from Charles Brasch's *Disputed Ground,* Basil Dowling's *Canterbury and Other Poems,* Keith Sinclair's *Strangers and Beasts,* and Colin Newbury's "In My Country" in *Landfall Country;* Paul's Book Arcade for lines from *Poetry of the Maori,* translated by Barry Mitcalfe; and Pegasus Press for lines from Denis Glover's *Arawata Bill.*

The photographs on pages 50, 107, and 134 are reproduced by courtesy of the National Geographic Society, Washington, D.C., and were first published in the *National Geographic Magazine* of April, 1962, in the feature "New Zealand: Gift of the Sea" with photographs by Brian Brake and text by Maurice Shadbolt.

E. Mervyn Taylor drew the tree-fern motifs used on pages 7, 58, and elsewhere, based on Maori rafter patterns, and the god-face pattern on page 39, based on a Maori wood carving. The photograph on page 57 is by John Clover, and was taken at the Alexander Turnbull Library, Wellington, by courtesy of the Librarian.

All Brian Brake's photographs were taken with 35-millimetre Leica and Nikon F cameras. The colour film used was Kodachrome I except in the case of the photograph on page 117, for which the film was High Speed Ektachrome exposed four hours for the glow-worms followed by a concealed-flash exposure to silhouette the boat. Monochrome film was Ilford HP3. UV filters were used exclusively, in all cases.